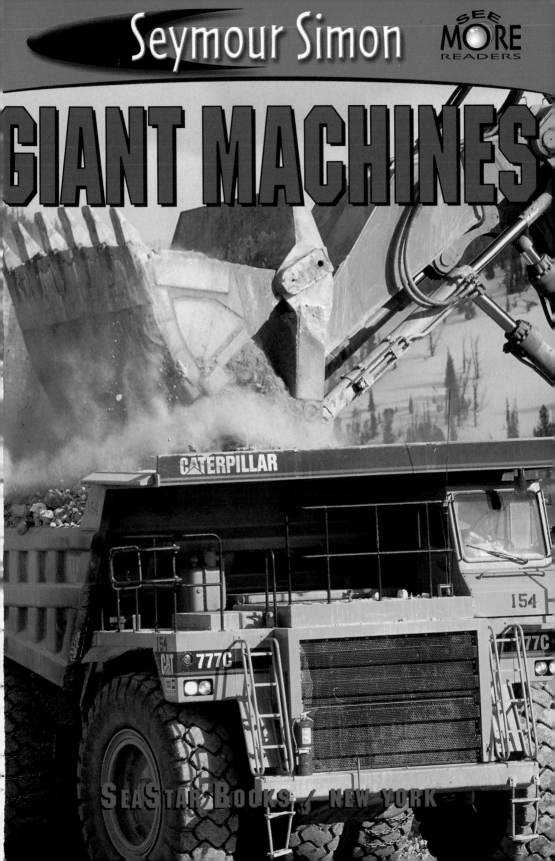

Seymour Simon

GIANT MACHINES

SeaStar Books / New York

To David Reuther,
with many thanks for his vision about this series.

Special thanks to reading consultant Dr. Linda B. Gambrell, Director of the School of Education at Clemson University, past president of the National Reading Conference, and past board member of the International Reading Association.

Permission to use the following photographs is gratefully acknowledged:
front cover, title page: © Dan Lamont/Corbis; pages 2–3, 30–31: © John Eastcott/YVA Momatiuk, Photo Researchers, Inc.; pages 4–5: © David Seawell/First Light; pages 6–7: © Komatsu Mining Systems; pages 8–9, 24–25: © Camerique/H. Armstrong Roberts; pages 10–11, 18–19: © W. Metzen/H. Armstrong Roberts; pages 12–13: Richard Hamilton Smith/Corbis; pages 14–15: © Paul Chesley/Tony Stone Images; pages 16–17: © Smith/Zefia/H. Armstrong Roberts; pages 20–21: © G. Ryan & S. Beyer/Tony Stone Images; pages 22–23: © Keith Wood/Tony Stone Images; pages 26–27: © M. Gibson/H. Armstrong Roberts; pages 28–29: © Mitch Kezar/Tony Stone Images; page 32: © Stephen Homer/First Light.

Library of Congress Cataloging-in-Publication Data is available.

ISBN 1-58717-126-0 (reinforced trade edition)
1 3 5 7 9 RTE 10 8 6 4 2
ISBN 1-58717-127-9 (paperback edition)
1 3 5 7 9 PB 10 8 6 4 2

PRINTED IN SINGAPORE BY TIEN WAH PRESS
For more information about our books, and the authors and artists who create them, visit our web site: www.northsouth.com

Giant machines help us do work.

This giant shovel
can move a mountain.
A giant earthmover
can carry a load that weighs
as much as 50 elephants.

This bulldozer blade

is as big as a billboard.

It can tear huge rocks

out of the ground,

or it can push trees aside.

One blade scoops up enough

dirt to fill a dump truck.

A scraper is like a shovel and
a wheelbarrow working together.
Scrapers cut up the ground
and carry the dirt away.

A front-end loader

lifts and moves dirt.

A giant loader can carry

a weight equal to that of

a big school bus.

This giant dump truck
is as tall and as wide
as a two-story house.
Its engine weighs
as much as four
pickup trucks.

Its tires are twice as tall

as a person.

This dragline is a giant crane with a digging bucket at the end.

In 50 days, a person with a shovel can dig a big hole. A dragline can dig that hole in one minute.

Bucket wheel excavators
scoop up huge amounts
of coal or dirt.
The largest excavators are
more than 600 feet long
and weigh nearly
30 million pounds.

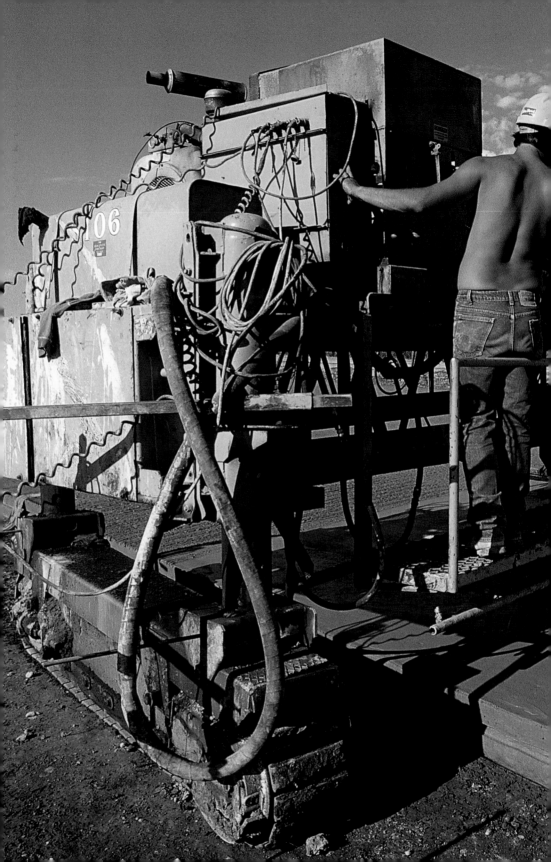

Pavers lay hot asphalt or
wet concrete onto the ground.

Then they flatten and smooth
it to make roads for cars
or runways for airplanes.

Tower cranes lift heavy loads
on skyscrapers, bridges,
shipyards, and mines.
These tower cranes
are 300 feet high,
the length of
a football field.

This offshore oil rig stands as tall as a skyscraper. It sits on legs that go 1,000 feet below the surface of the ocean. Giant cranes and drills pump thousands of barrels of oil a day.

This giant crawler carries a space shuttle to the launchpad at the Kennedy Space Center. The crawler travels at only one mile per hour. You can walk faster than that. But the crawler carries an 11–million–pound load.

A tub grinder
crushes boards
and wood waste.
Inside the tub,
huge steel wheels
smash the wood.
The chips
can be used
for fuel or mulch.

This 15-foot tub grinder
fills four big dump trucks
in one hour.

Farmers

use tractors

to pull machines

that help them

grow and harvest

their crops.

This tractor pulls

a cultivator that

cuts up weeds.

A combine cuts wheat,
corn, or bean plants.
In seconds, it separates
the crop from the stalks
and spits the grain or seeds
into a nearby truck.

A combine can harvest
100 acres of wheat a day.

Giant machines cut, carry, and move all kinds of things from one place to another. Next time you see a big machine, can you guess what it does?